Always Doing Being We Live Our Lives

Taiyu John Robertson

ISBN 978-0-6151-7295-8

Table of Contents

Pink Cloud

One of the things
people like me experience
is this sense of joy
that comes from the mere fact
of learning
we can go through a whole day
without getting drunk.

They call it a pink cloud
and its a cool deal.

Mine lasted eight months,
and ended the day
my son got sick.

There're any number
of realizations
people come to
or run from
as they crawl through their lives.

Some go down easy
while others
aren't so smooth.

This one was pretty damn tough,
and when I finally got home
from the hospital
and lay down
with that strange mix
of frantic won't sit still thought
and complete bone aching exhaustion,

my mind like a rolodex
flipped through one angry fear after the next,
until only the knowledge of how fragile
the most important part of my life had become
and always was
settled in,

and I finally came to rest
in the awareness
of how fucking bad
I needed to drink,
and how ashamed I was
at such a selfish thought.

With that,
the pink cloud
my life had become
those last few months,
came to an irrevocable
end.

Sunburn

Speaking of sunburns,
there was this one time
back in the 70s
when I went skinny dipping,
and got a terrible burn
on my dick.

It was bad enough
I should have gone
to the hospital.

And while there's nothing better
than swimming nekked and all,
I will never
under any circumstances
allow my genitals
to get sunburned again.

Not every bad thing's
like this, though
where once is enough
never to do it again.

With oysters,
it took two episodes
of puking and shitting
and six hours in the ER,
to get things figured out.

But when it came to rum,
that whole
don't do stuff that hurts
part of my brain
got shorted out,

because even after
a thousand mornings
of being sick
and shaking
and sweating
and stinking
and jittering myself
through the day,
with maybe three brain cells
still working,

once the sun headed west
all that mattered
was how thirsty
I was,

which is why
there has to be
something far more
than just remembering
jails,
divorces,
and driving home
with one eye closed night after night,
not to pick up again.

And Peace

There's really no way to describe
what it is to sit still
in zazen
and somehow for the very first time
find yourself
truly
letting go.

Its somehow
like an opening,
and pouring out

and in

where the feel of the cushion
and the sound of breathing
and the pressure there at the back of the neck
melts into the lighting up morning
punctured by the tire and motor noise
out on the road
as a train sounds again in the distance
all in a single simultaneous merging of sight and sound and thought
and peace.

Meatball

They wheeled him
into the procedure room
with the fork sticking out of his cheek
looking like a skewered meatball.

The surgeons administered two shots
and then simply pulled it out.

He was pissed, I suppose.
Anyone would be,
especially someone already consumed
with rage.

Across town,
the guy who did it
told the cop
if he had had another fork
he'd stick him again.

He was pissed, too,
though that particular river
ran far more shallow and uncertain
than the guy's in the hospital.

These stories
are real.
No names need changing,
because if you look hard enough
with an open heart,
you'll recognize the actors immediately.

They are the ones
just like everyone else.
You and me, for instance,
to name just two.

Its a small step,
you know,
from wherever you are
to wherever you go,
and though it seems
like a long trip
from way up in the air
to smack dab
on the ground,

the truth
tumbles faster
than the kicking screaming self
as the wind rushes past
right before
landing.

When Shakymuni Sat Under the Bodhi Tree

When Shakymuni sat under the bodhi tree
and saw the morning star,
time rolled on.

When Bodhidarma ripped off his eyelids
to ward away sleep,
the world still turned.

When Dogen raised the winter monastery
renewing the dharma
for all to breathe,
the wind blew hard and cold through the trees.

Last night
a storm rose up
and washed the streets clean
for the day.

Crickets

It sounds like a cowbell
clattering and clanking
us awake
there in that hall
before dawn.

Moving quickly,
except maybe the new ones,
who in uncertainty,
their minds rebelling
against the insane
clock,
flounder vacantly,
like fish in the shallows,

the bedding gone,
the cushions arranged
just so,
we sit and sway
and breathe
and wait.

In a moment
you hear the door open,
and the tell tale manner
of how he slips his feet
along the floor
comes to mind,
as everything else
gets real still.

There're still a few crickets,
grinding away
out in the wood,
while the cool breath
of the last of the night wind
cleanses
these tired faces.

Hearing him again,
knees to the floor
once, twice, thrice,
robes rustling quietly,
you wonder
where the crickets went.

Taking a breath,
sitting up straight
and high,
the thought occurs,
how young they are,
these new ones,
with minds so fresh
there's little chance yet
for clouds and pain
to take root,

as the Abbot moves
quietly on his morning rounds
along the rows.

And when his feet slip across
the wood floor
at your back,
you bow
in gratitude
for the chance

here in the dark
to come awake,

before turning again
to the crickets,
so graciously
waiting
for the bell,
before again resuming
their own
morning chant.

sleepless

don't get
these sleepless nights
much anymore

but got one now real good
when bone dead tired a while ago
I went to bed
and everything woke back up

wondering
does that to you,
and thinking,
remembering,
all the same thing

so you just go with it
like the unexpected
landslide
around that next curve
in the road

now its worrying
about being tired
tomorrow

and realizing
how much
of a little old man

I have become

Gangbanger

He jumped out a window
three years earlier
and never walked again.

Still lived at rehab
though the work
of learning how to roll yourself around
in a chair
was long over.

Some agency somewhere
kept promising
a new ride,
but it'd been months
and he remained planted
on borrowed wheels
they should have thrown out
three or four
patients earlier.

Came in every day
on the bus
with the others,
but while they
still had stuff to do,
he just hung out
by the entrance
smoking,

sitting in the shade,
a gangbanger
in a rusty wheelchair,
who couldn't read,
and didn't have no more friends,
and never had a job,
who always before kept going
on the hopes that came
from crack and pussy and hanging
with your buddies.

Them days were long gone,
which meant
he didn't face prison
or getting shot down in the street,
like in the future
he had before,

but this was way worse,
which is why
when his urine bag
exploded
all over the floor of my car,
I didn't mind

though the smell came back
on humid summer days
and then he'd be in my mind
for the rest
of whatever trip
I was on.

Suchness

You see
the problem
for most
is that
all these solutions
involve some new salve
to treat
the incurable
fact
of being
a human being,

which itself
just is,
and thereby
doesn't need
medicine.

So, you might

want to put
down brokenness,
and let loose
clinging itself,

opening the heart instead
to sound of birds
and the cool breeze
of a boundless moon.

The Conceit of Conceits

They say somehow
we're different.

They believe
we have *character defects*
which caused us to do
the bad things we did,
that we were selfish and self centered,
angry and resentful.

There's others out there,
so it goes,
who don't have such difficulties,
aren't over sensitive,
didn't run on fear,
and get to drink normally,
whatever that means.

Our's is a lack
of power
to manage lives,
handle stress,
and navigate choppy seas,
they claim.

Which makes us special
in our grandiosity,
because the
God-of-our-own-understanding

graces

such miserable creatures

as us

with the undeserved gift

of redemption,

eviscerating the craving

and handing back

our lives.

And when such talk

runs strong and loud,

I have learned

to hunker down

and ride it out,

because,

in me,

there resides

no such gloom,

certitude,

nor pride.

The Illinois State Fair

We'd scrounge together our nickels and dimes
and like little beggars
get someone to drive us down to the fair grounds
every day
for two weeks
each August.

We'd sneak in
right behind the midway,
and from there,
it was a short walk
to the Rock O Plane,
the Zipper,
and the Double Ferris Wheel.

They even had strippers,
but only one of us
ever had the nerve
to check that tent out.

We'd lounge around
in the grass
with real hippies,
smoke cigarettes,
and sometimes go see a concert,
though that meant an extra admission.

Nixon came one year, and brought state troopers with rifles
who watched from the roof
of the Illinois Building,
as he rode by on his way to the election.

And the Who showed up
to open for the Association
on the stage by the stock car race track,
though we didn't know who they were
until years later.

We were children
and this all was magic,
and every year after it ended
we made a vow
for the next,

knowing
nothing would ever change
in the endless cycle
of innocence
our lives had become.

Girls Gone Wild

I saw the Girls Gone Wild tour bus blocking the road
that night in the rain,
but figured it just broke down or something.

The next day the paper said
they hit a homeless guy on a bike,
and he was probably drunk,
and thus somehow
deserved to be run over.

Turned out to be Bill,
with the little dog Buddy,
and the best lame excuses
for why he had
to go back out.

We heard they took his leg off
right there in the street
and sealed up the wound
so he couldn't bleed out
when they pulled him free.

Three weeks later
he escaped from the hospital
and came across the street to see us
in a wheelchair with his beepers and plugs
and hoses and wires.

It wasn't pretty.
He moaned and coughed
and bitched about the *whore bus*,
and when he showed us where his leg used to be
everyone got a little queasy.

I took him back to the hospital around one in the morning
listening all the way
while he rattled on about what happened,
before finally confessing
not to remember a thing from an hour before
until three days later.

I wonder what its like
waking up
and finding your leg gone?

A Brightly Lit and Squishy Core

Its the fallen ones
I connect with best,
the broken and doomed
always more alive
to the grit and sweet smells
of the universe.

Maybe its because I'm not exactly
a day at the beach either,
or maybe because this here ego
is all full of itself
and likes to think it saves others
for sport.

But I prefer to believe,
instead maybe,
that in those
whose lives
have been less than stellar,
and whose
struggle it is
just to get through the day
without making more a mess of things
then they started out with,

there is a common core
of faith and hope
that them others,

you know,
the ones with all the stuff
and the pretty precocious children
and the money
and the future
and the appearance
of contentment,

refuse to see

and therefore
take for granted.

There is always
a brightly lit and squishy core
in these aching longing hearts
where everything resides
more clear and pure

than anywhere else
in the universe.

And once opened
to finally see
how nothing's really broken,
these formerly clumsy stupid
ugly sad and dangerous beings,
like me,

well, they go on
to light the path
for all the rest of us
to finally make our way
home
from the night.

The Weight

Everything has always been
heavier for me,
than it should have been.

The bad times were just a little worse
and the good not quite as good
as for others.

Coming awake again
after finding and leaving behind the antidote,
that weight has returned,

though now
the difference is
that such thoughts
of heavy or light
are somehow less important
than they were
when life itself
depended upon them.

The Coffee Pot From Hell

I had this coffee maker
that puked up water and grounds
all over the counter
about as often as it made coffee right,
and when the thing didn't work,
it usually being around 6:30 or so in the morning
and me not exactly intact and up to speed
because I hadn't had my morning coffee and all,
you'd know because I'd be cussing and screaming and wanting
to break stuff.

Kept the thing for years though,
always expecting it to do a better job
than its capability allowed,
thinking how if I got the filter
just right,
or poured the water correctly,
or put the grounds in evenly,
or unevenly,
or whatever,
that it would do
what I thought
it was supposed to do
all along
for me.

So tonight I was thinking
how that's also
the way I am
with other human beings.

expecting they do what I think they ought to do

for me

and getting pissed off when they don't.

Eventually I tossed the coffee pot from hell,

went online and found one

17 other people on Amazon

said actually worked.

So far,

its only puked twice.

But you can't really toss out other people,

because they deserve better

and unlike the coffee pot

aren't supposed to be

predictable.

And anyway,

people aren't tools,

much less my tools.

So at this point,

the metaphor breaks down,

doesn't it?

The Cushion and the Bell

I thought I required deliverance
and chased rainbows
for salvation
until such time
as it became finally clear
just how far you can run
without moving an inch.

Now that there is nothing to get
and glimpsing the shadow of needlessness,
all that's left
is the cushion
and the bell.

Hungry Ghosts

There isn't a day gone by
when I haven't wanted to do something
to change the way I think and feel.

Which makes me no different
than anyone else,
I suppose.

We hungry ghosts
aren't exactly
a rare breed.

They Were Glory Days

They were glory days
right out of college
paying bills
living with my lover
learning what it is
to be all grown up.

It lasted a few years,
she and I,
and as true as that love was,
something happened
and I got scared
and after that
the walls closed in
and it was time to leave,
again.

I found her two decades later,
when I was feeling sorry for myself
and wanting to pick old wounds.

She said she hadn't done so well at first,
but later got it together,
finished school,
married twice
and lives way up north near Canada.

When I tried to tell her how awful
I knew I'd been,
she agreed
and laughed
about how long ago
all that was.

I wish now
I'd been able
to measure myself up,
back then
when it mattered,

because truth be told
I still love her

same as always.

Only profound To Me

She said
the thing that hurts
isn't love.

Because love isn't
a thing
at all.

I said,
say that again
so I can write it down,
which embarrassed her.

Then I said,
I think that may be
the most profound thing
I ever heard.

She looked at me
like I was nuts.

Maybe its only profound
to me.

Nothing

Having heard much,
I have now seen a little.

And having now
seen a little,
I have attained nothing.

Six Stories

everyone's got about six stories to tell
over and over
which makes it nice
when someone new
wanders into your life

so you can tell yours
and they can tell theirs

and only the ones who've heard it all before
get torqued off

mine are pretty tiresome

but you dance with what brung ya

right?

Dharma Name

I have this dharma name
my teacher gave me
when I became
a Buddhist

It refers to serenity
which he knows
I lack

and wisdom
which he hopes
I get

We'll see

Just For The Moment

I'd be lying
if I said
I didn't miss the chaos and excitement
just a little.

There's nothing quite like
the sublime hazy euphoria
of a good drunken stupor
where nothing matters
and everything's funny
and you don't care what happens
so long as its over the top,
rough,
and nasty.

Its interesting
how the times when I miss it the most
are the times

when I'm worn down
with sadness,

and feel a need
to escape my own skin
just for the moment.

stooped shoulders

its not that this here suitcase
of pain
isn't real,

its just that
me having it
isn't necessary.

flowing, as such things do,
from the sharp edged habits
of old old mind,

coming up
out of the depths
of childhood's end times,

where you learn but can't speak
of how the big people
weren't gods,
and the weight
of history
bears down more and more
on stooped shoulders.

these delusions
don't exactly
flee the coop
just because the door's open.
not with all them wolves
still lurking nearby.

not yet at least,
which explains
why the baggage
still comes with the grown man
i have become.

i still hear the howling
and can't sleep sometimes
with my feet hanging off
the edges
of the bed.

40s

You want to come downtown with me
to hang with the drunks and beggars
and thems that's sick in the head?

They stink a little
and talk real loud
to no one in particular
as they shuffle around,
or shake and twitch,
or swish and cackle,
so that it seems like
you ought to be scared,

though hardly anyone
from the outside
ever gets hurt.

If you come early
and make a friend or two,
maybe buy a couple of 40s
and share your smokes,
you'll find new truth
that never dawned
even a single minute before.

We'll end up
under one of the bridges drinking
and eventually maybe sleeping,

and if the weather's warm,
its possible
to talk yourself
into believing there's freedom
in laying out and staring at the stars
like this,

at least until the asshole teenage cops
decide how fun it'd be
to check us out
and see
who loses it first
and has to go to jail.

If you're willing, though
to shit your pants
every day or so no matter what,
they leave you alone
regardless of what you do.

That's a trick
our newer
piss and vinegar brothers
haven't figured out
quite yet.

All Along

What about you?

Did you find peace?

Is *now*
what you expected
way back
when they taught
how life was fair and right?

Or, is
the this
life became

more complicated,

so that by the time
you get untwisted enough
to wonder at all,

more pressing concerns
emerge.

In fact, I bet,
even the mere suggestion
lurking therein,
makes your thinking speed up
and the little gut heaving
sick feeling
kick in,

blocking clarity,
making excuses,

just like when you they ask

Are you happy?

Was love found?

And, how'd it go,
that life well lived?

No matter,

thinking about this stuff
falls by the curb pretty fast

what with the way
things turned.

That's how it was with me,
until the mess was just too much
to ignore,

and these fucking questions
had to be asked.

Everything Else Was Gorgeous Deep Royal Blue

So this deal happened
a few years ago
one morning
when I was up bumbling around
hungover and slurping coffee

There on TV
the big New York building
was on fire
and they were saying something about
a plane crash,

which didn't surprise me,
since I knew them towers
went pretty high up.

I sipped coffee
and watched,
and saw this other plane
fly into
the other tower,

and thought how absolutely incredible it was
that in a single day
the same kind
of accident
could happen
twice like that.

I mean, the odds against
such a thing
were simply astounding
proving yet again
how crazy bizarre
life can be.

Then the towers came down
and that dirt cloud wall
filled Manhattan
and they figured out
what was really up.

It still took awhile
to soak into this thick skull.

Later that day
driving home
under the huge blank sky,
I realized
deep down in the gut
how, with what had happened,

nothing
anymore
would
ever be the same
again.

There were three contrails
above my head,
and you could tell
whoever it was
was flying real real low.

Everything else
was gorgeous
deep royal blue.

We watched TV
pretty much around the clock
for the next month or so,
seeing again and again
them guys jumping out windows

and everyone else
running from the inconceivable horror
their lives had become.

Since then,
and though I suppose
its all understandable,
we ultimately missed
a chance,

slipping back instead
to angry denial
about the reality
of transitory life,

which is why
the whole thing now
is just bad bad people
somewhere else
needing to die,

while they plan
the spectacle
they're going to fill
that hole in the ground with

where a part
of each of us
now lies.

The Water Itself

there has always
been
this sense
of unease

that like clockwork
explodes
into an unfathomable pain

upon the realization
that whatever
had been working
quit

and the suffering

was back

where all I can think
is how awful
stuff's going to be
until something new
crowds it out

now
at my best
I don't every time run
for each new shadow
quite so fast

but instead feel
the waves
cover my head
and push me down
into the cold womb
of the deep sea

where eventually
you fade
into the water itself
and merge quietly
into everything there is.

Walnuts

These walnuts
fallen by the thousands
from stately towering monoliths
each carry everything needed
to recreate
the whole world
in the blink of an eye.

My blackened hands
taste sweet
as we fill
crate after crate
with seeds
of future life.

And years from now
a forest may grow
where fields of corn once lay,

though for now
collected fruit
is all there is.

Tightrope

Its like being a tightrope walker
standing on your hands
on a bicycle
out on the wire
balanced just so
above a cruel crowd

with people
at each end
on little platforms
tossing out more balls
and pins
and flaming torches
for you to juggle.

Most important
though,
isn't any of this,
but the fact
that as you wobble around out there

all you can think of
is how you probably can't do it
and what'll happen
when you fail,

and what the crowd will think
when the inevitable happens,
at any moment now.

That Felt Emptiness Remains

I used to believe
there was a huge hole
in my heart
that needed filling.

That isn't how I see it anymore,
even though that felt emptiness
remains.

Its different now
because what I thought was a hole
is really just sadness
that I don't much like.

It sparked up tonight
when I saw some old photos
of my son

back when he was two,
with a big pudgy innocent face
and curious deep eyes,

which brought back a time
where I was still able to pretend
everything could be good
between me and his mom.

It didn't work out
like anyone planned;
what with her crawling inside wherever she'd go
even deeper than anyone thought possible,

and me disappearing
to the bars,

all of which was incredibly selfish
for both of us,
because he didn't need
to learn this shit
quite so young.

There's a whole ocean of water
gone under the bridge
that connects us all
in desperate love
from those times,

and I still have this ache,
coming in fits and starts
up from the sub flooring
in my belly.

Which is why,
though it seems like a hole
where a big eyed kid
peers out,

its not really
empty at all.

Not the Boat

Not in the boat,
but the boat itself.

Not the boat,
but the stream itself.

Not the stream,
the water.

Not the water,
the world.

Not the world,

the universe,

and not the universe
at all.

Converging Paths

She was who I needed
when nearly everything in my life
was terrible,

where all I knew to do
was stay the course
no matter how bad it got.

We walked
converging paths.

Mine was hedonistic and destructive and lonely,
a rebellion against the pressure
of trying to be
and failing.

Hers was lonely too,
and sacrificial
and open, and alive.

I guess I gave her a way
to safely let
the bad girl out,

though it wasn't really safe at all,
because if you're diabetic,
its probably not a good idea
to try and keep up
with my drinking
for two years.

She did all right though,
and we filled what we thought
were the empty places
in each other's hearts,

but after I got sober
what I thought I needed
changed.

That was a good thing too;
she'd have never finished
the dissertation
without me running out.

Chrome

A puff of smoke
      on a windy day.

A shining jewel
      under a full moon.

Burning bright and hot
      against cold night air.

      as chrome light

      illumes
      the shadows
      on a once dark path.

What we once thought
      were clouds,
      was only steam
      from far too many words.

Smooth As Ice

Its not about being
free of pain.

Its not about bread
and circuses
and a free t shirt,
either.

This life
becomes
what it already is,

every moment
bleeding into the next,
flowing,
churning,
wet and sloppy,
smooth as ice.

Whatever.

Fluffy Pink Easter Bunnies

There's a crashing roaring sound
your ears almost hear
when the shit hits the fan
and that old familiar thud
lands square in your belly,
where the doom lives and feasts
on the fodder of craving,
upon which, in turn,
sore tired egos
so desperately depend.

And though all this -
every last speck -
is no more real
than the fluffiest pink Easter bunny
dancing gaily across some warm April lawn,

for such learning
there is no teacher
but life itself

and time.

Plague

Back in the day
he was a world class forger,
before the feds showed up
and the plague kicked in.

It was years later
when we met;
he just looked scared,
wearing orange
and sitting in the cheap plastic chair.

We got him out of jail
and back on the cocktail,
but after all that time
pretending everything was fine,
it was all a day late
and a dollar short.

So when he showed up again this week,
slumped over
there in the wheelchair
with the nurse dabbing at the sores and puke
on his face,
you could tell
he wasn't long for this world.

That night,
while I sat
in the zendo
on my cushion
in the dark,
he kept coming back,

along with James,
and Larry,
and all the other dead.

They sat with me,
backs straight,
hands just so,

until the bell rang
and we drove home
on wet glass streets
of red and green.

The Kind of Love That Cries

When its all said and done
and they scrape the ashes out of the oven
and hand the urn over
to whoever shows up with the check

there won't be many tears shed
for me.

Some folks just don't generate
those kind of sentiments,

and I'm one of them.

I wish it were different,
but truth be told
though I certainly do my share
of good deeds,

the kind of love that cries and mourns
isn't there for me.

Absolutely Nuts

I don't know what love is any more,
but what I used to think it was
I've had plenty of.

Its an achy longing
and jumpy heart thing
where whatever she says and does
is beautiful,

where you don't mind
letting your yous
merge,

and where every time
there's a move towards her

she also moves
towards you,

such that your lives
seem to somehow
become
not two.

Now that kind of thing
has happened to me
to one degree
or another
many times,

and in a very big way
once,

although that time
ended badly,
after years
of one of us always moving
forward,
and the other running
away.

Which leaves
a part of me now
quite bit later
still in love,
afraid to cozy up,

and thinking
whatever it is
love is
is absolutely
nuts.

The Karma You Seek

People talk about chickens
being so stupid
they stand outside
in the rain
looking up
until they drown,

but I'm not so sure
that's much different
than what people do.

And of course,
while who knows
ultimately
the reasons
why anyone does
what anyone does,

even chickens,

there is an old saying
that if you want to know
what your karma's gonna be,
just look around
at life right now
and maybe there
you'll find a clue.

So if you see yourself
coughing and choking
on the measure of life
that's come your way,

with the rain
quietly
filling your belly,

than maybe
looking to the sky
for whatever it is
that is,
isn't the answer.

Nothing Wrong

People get nervous
when you suggest
there's nothing wrong with them.

They want character defects
and imperfections,
problems
and issues,

I think, because they know
there's a painful disconnect
between what is
and what they've been told
ought to be.

And since they know
the whole blame thing

gets pretty childish after awhile,

that just leaves one other person,
as the cause
of their demise.

night terrors

A throbbing whooshing sound came every night
along with the sense
that I was being sucked backwards
through a tunnel
to a pulsing pumping beat

This imagery of mind
brought on a vivid delusion
of huge throbbing machinery
and people with small heads
a thousand miles away

Crying out
my father would come
and carry me into my parents' bed
where, trembling and shaking
until the spell passed,
I'd finally lapse
into exhausted sleep

Well into adulthood now,
on occasion
the terror still comes around
to drag me away
into a world of machines and fear.

But I'm not afraid

Not anymore.

Who's to Say?

Who's to say
the day before

the flower not blossomed
wasn't?

There in mud
all things
already are.

Discipline

The discipline
of waking in the dark,
dressing quietly,
and driving across town
to sit
an hour before the sunrise
is not something
I am used to.

But then,
hard pressed as always
to identify anything
not immediately gratifying
which doesn't require
some sort of internal cajoling

I climb from bed
and gather up
the rakasu.

The Best Part

When you're a drunk in your cups
the world shrinks down
to whatever there is
within a very small circle
that ends
about a foot from your face.

And, to what you hear
from whoever gets in close enough
to overcome
the pulsing throbbing buzz
roaring between your ears.

And although you like to think
the best part's at the beginning
of the night
when you can still walk and talk,
in truth
its when you finally
get home and pass out

and thereby know
you did it again
got away with something
one more time

and escaped
from whatever it is
lurking just around the corner
always barely out of sight

though vigilant and ready
to snap you in half
at the slightest
miscalculation.

My Steel Cage

I came to see
what I thought was freedom
turns out was just rust,
covered in crusty
blood and dried puke.

And while before
I thought the armor
could be removed safely enough,
now there's the realization
it ain't so easy stripping down
to raw throbbing skin.

I did finally get it off.
Its in the closet nearby,
sometimes very nearby,

and ever since
I have scrubbed and bleached and soaked myself
to try and remove the stains.

While most have faded,
when its hot out
and there's no wind,
the smell comes back,

as do the scars
left years ago
by the workings
of that steel cage.

Candle

I couldn't help her.
I couldn't free her pain.
I couldn't even make things easier or better or softer.

I failed,
though the trying,
a significant monumental endeavor
filled with struggle
and determination
and sweat
and sacrifice,
went on forever.

I even tried not trying,
and there too
found the same
no good end.

Even then, though alone
and long gone left behind,
I still kept the candle lit
and the door unlocked

until yet again
having crashed and burned,
a bloody heart smashed flat
against smooth worn rock,

and finally believing
myself redeemed,
in thinking's wishful clarity,
from these stupid foolish
desperate times,

I vowed with all beings
to let go the clinging
and send these puffs of pretty smoke
from that ever burning candle
skyward to the wind

When Katagiri Died

When Katagiri died
there was this sense
of incompletion

lingering above the smoke and scent
of mourning and sadness.

And through the years
the ghosts of that time,
those sensibilities,
these half full bowls

still rear up
in the eyes of the heirs
as they work tirelessly
planting flowers,
all around the world.

Chunks

By the time I finally came to terms
with what a disaster drinking had become
it was too late
and I couldn't stop.

A few years later,
still at it
and the pain unbearable,
there was this sense of miserable doom
where only at the end
did the thought of giving it up
become only slightly less horrible
than the thought of staying out
even one more day.

Now its a couple of more years down the road;
I been sober the whole time,
not counting cigarettes and coffee,
and through the ebb and flow
certain truths seem to float up to the surface
over and over again.

Learning to go through a day without drinking
isn't as hard as I thought it'd be;
the mere act of abstaining from alcohol
is the easiest part of this here project.

Its too bad the euphoria
of that realization
doesn't last.

But you can't begin to get at
the real problem
until the stuff that made drinking
seem like such a good idea in the first place
rears up and begins banging on the bars.

That's when most people
just go back out.

Funny thing is,
the churning chunky deep down stuff
that's so terrifying,
isn't real.

Not really.
At least not in the way you think.

But you can't tell that
to the guy who's in a panic
because the voices in his head
are screaming
and the angry depressed worrying
has him by the nuts again.

And although all you have to do
to get through it
is not drink no matter what,
and open your heart just a little
to the what really is
of the universe,

there aren't that many people
who'll choose real healing
over drinking,
or any of its lesser included
evils.

Done Needing Coffee

I go to this coffee shop about every day
around four thirty or so.

Its always full
of regulars
who're studying
or chatting
and every once in awhile
taking a drink of something hot.

There's nothing funky about the place;
even the furniture is a studied exercise
in coffee culture.

I got hit on in there once
by a woman who liked
how big my computer was.

But when I told her I didn't drink,
the conversation
abruptly
ended.

Or maybe the whole thing
was wishful thinking.

There's a guy alone in the corner, tonight
with the fish aquarium,
the new roommate,
the holiday trip to Des Moines,
soooo much to do before Thursday,
and the wireless cell phone earpiece and microphone,
pissing people off.

And another guy,
older,
balding and grim,
with a perfectly weathered
leather jacket
who doesn't like the aquarium roommate cell phone guy
one bit.

I can't keep my eyes
off the Chinese girl
two tables down,
with the blinky smiling eyes
drinking water and talking intently
to her lover.

She just walked by,
with the happy smug look
20 something love
gives you.

I'm done needing caffeine
and gather up my things,
before heading out into the dusky evening.

There Was Me

This business of letting down your guard
and opening your hands
to make a place
upon which the world may rest
has captured my attention
tonight.

Once, yesterday
as I was walking across the garage
from my car
to the elevator,
I looked up from the scenes and voices
in my head
to notice how everything there
was me.

The concrete floor
and low hard ceiling,
the light and sound,
the cool dry air.

And tonight, with that recollection
I felt more than thought
how much larger and vastly different
self is
than any mere ego
could ever imagine.

The Sound

I want to be
one who no longer
employs a grand strategy in life.

I want to be one
who gives up
the counselor dude and the big bad biker
and the problem solving son of a bitch
that thinks the path lies through the swamp
of your approval.

I seen too much wreckage
and desperate struggle
to believe any longer
in some master plan
for me or you or anyone else.

So now instead
I just want to be,
and in that place
listen closely
for the free flowing sound
of the universe
unfolding
without hindrance
in this old broken heart.

Good Enough For Now

I have not loved
like I wished
any of my wives
and girlfriends
and best friends
and strangers.

And though there was always
compassion
and joy
and delight
in their beauty and grace
and passion,

there was also
always a neediness,
in the same sense
that I needed a cigarette
or a drink
or a thing
that reached me out to them

to fix me up,
and smooth things over
and give the rush
or the comfort
or whatever the hell else
was needed
at the time.

It ain't like now I'm all better or anything,

but not being any worse

is good enough

most of the time.

Oceans

There's no way
to understand
anything
about the ocean
simply standing in the shallows
thinking
this is all there is.

Which is probably why
the thing
I thought
I was

clumsily mindlessly
staggered
through life
careening

from one redemption
to the next,
always
searching for sandy beaches
and cool blue shade.

Until the smallest thing
I thought
was all
I was

dived headlong
into the immense hungry ghost
of drinking life
seeking,
craving,
wallowing,
and begging,

until finally
he collapsed
in tears and agony,
sensing somehow
after no unturned rock remained,

that indeed,
no unturned rock remained.

And although
merely knowing
in itself,
don't change much,
you gotta start
somewhere.

That night
after that last wave crashed
over this weeping bloody face,

the surf finally somehow
came into view,
and my gaze
began to sweep beyond,
to the vast deep unknown
stretching endlessly
towards the moon

and the thing
I thought was all I was
began to fade
into the misty depths.

Karmic Eyes

There's supreme karmic irony
at work here, you know
in the realization
that finally
after all these years
of clumsy struggle,

when I'm able
to shine a bit of light
out of these dusty wrinkled eyes,
and lure smooth loving bodies
and bright laughing minds
to lay with me
under heavy warm covers,

the truth is
I'm pretty much
no longer willing
to set aside
whatever it is
I am now,

in service
to that fifteen year old
horny lonely geeky guy
that just wants
to get laid,

who lives
within this gray haired
aging man
with the twinkly eyes,
and the wicked grin.

Which means
the compulsion
for sex
has given way
to the desire
for love,

which you can't do
if either party
is just
an object.

The Spit Pit

I was going into the 8th grade
at a new school
in a new town.

It was a bad time,
where, looking back,
the sadness that became
my closest friend
and constant companion,
first introduced itself.

The school was big and red bricked
and depressing,
up there on the hill
at the dead end.

And though we'd moved so often
that making friends
was second nature,
here, where no one ever came or went,
it was somehow different.

They had an asphalt yard
along the front of the building,
and a sunken stairwell
leading down to the shop room.

It was called the spit pit,
where kids who didn't fit in
got thrown,
whenever the mood struck.

I got grabbed
that first week,
by three or four other boys
who thought because I was new
I must be a pussy.

They were right,
but not so much
that I couldn't fight.

After a minute or so, they gave up,
though the leader of that little pack
said I had to meet him
after school,
one on one,
to settle things.

They grabbed a smaller kid
and when it was over
he crawled out
covered in spit and tears
and shame.

I hated that school
and that town
and those assholes.

After class, the kid who wanted to fight me
didn't show,
never mentioned it again,
and neither did I.

We ended up buddies,
smoking pot and
drinking cherry vodka together
every weekend.

He still has
my Allman Brothers at the Fillmore East.
I thought of that a couple of years ago
when I was back there
and saw him at the McDonalds.

Its funny
how some stuff
you never forget.

The Cliff I Know

Its desire itself
they crave,
these lonely
self absorbed
people.

Its the filled up
sated oozing over the top
sensation
that fuels their struggle.

With drink
and smoke
and food
and lust,

they seek to fill
the unexamined hole
they think lies
at the base of the cliff
from whence they jumped,
a long long time ago.

I know.
Believe me,
I know.

Exploding Buddha

They blew up
the ancient giant Buddhas
carved out of
those bluffs
there in Afghanistan
a few years ago.

It was a terrible thing
done in hate and arrogance,
said the Christians
about the loss.

The Buddha
would not,
presumably,
share that sentiment.

Hells bells;
the Buddha would have probably
helped place
the dynamite.

Does the Moon Cry?

I wonder what its like
being taken for granted
like the moon?

Existing everywhere
Cool gray light and shadows

unnoticed
by so many
who day after day
never see
past the hollow
at the base
of pulsing skulls.

Does the moon cry
in heaving sobs,
or quietly,

like mourning
that lasts
forever?

Undone Flowers

when they laid the teacher down
in fiery kiln on concrete floor
grieving silent
upright undone flowers
carried the news

with the deepest sadness
anyone could ever imagine

years later
ashes and black robes
spread themselves
across cold fields
of corn and concrete

opening hearts
to the moment
that never ends

All of Which

When you quit thinking
about yourself
every fucking waking minute

you also stop feeling
so bad or angry
or depressed
or anxious.

When you let go
of the stuff
that messed you up
way back
when it was all supposed to be easy and innocent,
even cooler shit happens.

And since
only a very small part
of tomorrow
needs attending right now,
that squalling, too
begins to fade.

All of which,
if nothing else,
makes for one hell
of a lot more
present moment
here
and now.

christmas turds

christmas
was the only time
everyone might come home

we'd eat and laugh
and pretend to be
a normal family
for a day or two

before the smell
from the stinking turds
just got too damn strong

then the anger and fear
came boiling over
and they'd all disappear again

until next year
or the next decade

for the longest time
I didn't know anything
about why this was our way

only after thirty years
did the dots connect
the bubble pop
and I could see
the reasons
for our karma

Frozen Trail

Around the time of cold solstice
the tipping point
shifts downward
like after when a rocket burns out.

Then, trees and bushes
somehow know
to start cooking up the stuff
that makes green happen.

Before, with the world seemingly
locked down
in frozen custard slumber,
nothing drips or spreads
too far beyond
where it started,

as you crunch around
trying not to slip too far
and topple over.

And unless care's taken,
its almost like not living at all.

But then the green thing begins,
so quiet and subtle
as to go unnoticed

until in a wonderful
pig stink dawn,
everything gets lurid
and lush
and wet
and bright.

And you think
this is it,
as opposed to that
which somehow wasn't,
back down the frozen trail
into the dark.

Not Even A Bad Thing

I'd get an itch
you just can't scratch
and go out
seeking.

There'd be no telling
what I'd find,
though no doubt
it'd not be good enough
in the long run.

There then came
an awareness,
albeit foggy and uncertain,
that the sound
of an unrung bell
isn't a problem to be solved

nor a bad thing
needing changing.

Everything

Every once in awhile
something happens
where everything changes
and you just know
from there on out
the world
will forever be
a different place.

The last was when
my boy got sick
which followed close on the heels
of getting sober,
after coming home from jail
which in turn,
began the end
of the years of hungry ghosts.

These changes happen
just as often
in more pleasant ways,
like when David was born,
or when I realized
who I wanted
to spend the rest of my life with.

Ultimately
there's no telling
which is a good thing and which isn't,

though my boy not needing insulin every day
just to survive
might be that rule's
exception.

So It Becomes You

The river ran fast, cold,
and clean,
all the way to the gravel and sand bottom.

Spring fed for most of its length,
it flowed strong
even in August
when everything else was all dried up.

Like most,
it'd ease along all calm and gentle
until the next bend,
only to rear up and get white and loud,
sometimes branching into narrow channels,
cluttered by rocks and twists,

then crashing and tumbling down
before finding its legs,
and smoothing out again
for awhile.

If you weren't careful,
you'd dump there in the rough,
and like the trees and branches we'd see along the way,
jam up and drown
in the crystal clear
rushing cold.

The other choice
meant melting your canoe
into the current
and floating along
like the water itself,

twisting and turning with the waves,
moving in the current,
barely leaving a mark
on the rippling surface behind you.

If done right,
the fast white turns and drops
were just places to coast
without concern,

not tiring,
not fighting,
letting the gap
between you and the river
melt.

And maybe
just as much as you became
it,
so it
became
you.

That's the secret,
you know.

Not fighting,
nor going limp,
just joining in,
and with,

so that the flowing of the water
becomes the flowing
of your heart.

This is the Prayer

This is the prayer
for all sentient beings
finding peace
in a world
of truth and light.

This is the prayer
for the trees and grasses,
rustling in the wind,
and still
at dawn.

This is the prayer
for beggars and thieves,
to find their path
of scented flowers
and dreams like clouds.

This is the prayer,
for the blind and deaf,
whose hearts might finally open
in these fleeting days.

And this is a prayer

for the one in gassho
to realize
the heart within

filled as it is
with trees and grasses,
beggars and thieves,
the blind and deaf.

May all we are,
and all we become,
sit quietly in peace
under a full and silver moon.

What Amnesiacs Know

Sometimes I think all I am
is a clusterfuck
of mindless habits
and reactions
cycling monotonously
from one damn thing
to the next.

And the only thing
stringing it all together
is this tendency
to believe that
because I remember stuff,
there must be a me
underneath
it all

sort of like overused flypaper
connecting its victims
into one large
dead
organism.

Makes you wonder
if amnesiacs
get it right
all along.

deluded

There
in the space
between

this

and thought

lies the true dharma moment
that eludes we
deluded

who struggle on
like starving fools
at the banquet.

blood or bile

there must be a fever because
i'm having some
damn weird dreams
and cranking the thermostat
up and down all the time

yesterday
i was coughing up
something soupy
into the back of the throat

tomorrow for all i know
there'll be blood
or bile

a friend told me
how it is with her
how she can't take
emotional or physical pain

and all i had to say
in a dried up squeaky voice
was how it damn sure
seemed that way

though if i had her phone number
i'd call and tell her
stuff only hurts too much
when you can't see a path
through it

The Feeling of Miracles

You don't have to confuse
the feeling
of miracles
with the real thing.

Karma
isn't the same
as destiny.

Things might seem
like they happen
for a reason,

but that's just ego
stepping out
for a night on the town.

Don't Need No Caffeine Anymore

This new day
wakes up
fresh, cold, and crisp,

finds me
overslept
congested
just going
through the motions.

Still talking
the right things
but tired
less willing
to see out
other's eyes.

Missing my boy
as always,
clinging,
winding me
out of step,

and wishing
these fucking voices
would just this once
take a smoke break
or something.

Even the coffee shop music
is too loud
just as well
don't need
no caffeine
anymore.

Very Very Good And Never Ever Enough

You can't be a real poet
till you write something pithy
about first love.

Mine was juicy like peaches
with warm wet aching lips
and buttercup cow eyes big as hubcaps.

Had the patience
of a mountain
but so always gentle
you never noticed
the bending.

Still don't know what love is
but what I had for her
well that was something
very very good
and never ever enough.

The Horses

And then she talked about
smoking crack all the time
while they watched the horses die,

dragging them away to burn
because you can't just leave
dead horses
lying around
on your property like that.

But they couldn't do much more
because the truck wouldn't run
and the power got turned off
so the well didn't pump
and they had to live
like the animals
that died.

Even after the government took the children
they couldn't put down their pipe;

hell, that made things worse.

Still does,

and left me wondering
how in god's name
do you ever get past
something like that?

its the bell

Every morning when we sit
on black candle lit cushions
in that darkened zendo

it starts in echoing silence
where all there is
is breathing and straight backs

stretching the seconds into centuries
or popping like soap bubbles,
depending on who knows why.

Sometimes there's a floating
peaceful thing,
where you easily drift along a bit
before noticing and gently paddling back
to the wall and the floor,
over and over.

Or, from the first moment
your knees scream
and your brain howls
and every click
of that imaginary fluttering clock
up in the corner

ticks

along

like

dripping

sap.

You always know when its about over, though
either because the crows appear,
starting from somewhere
behind and distant
and ending just the opposite

or because the old ones
there in the room
around you,
can't keep
from creaking and shifting
anymore.

Either way,

its the bell
that ends this one thing
and starts the next.

Koan

No longer possessing the easy luxury
of judgmental arrogance
or the ego of the graced
or doomed,
I have found the chance
for real compassion
almost within
arm's reach.

Certainty isn't,
nor the written truths of other people,
the claims of elders,
and the pretty smoke and bells
signaling something momentous
about to occur,

though in all things
there lies dharma,

especially once
you see the path
by nature
travels
through unknown peaks
and fog filled valleys.

The Most Sublime

This one's for the elders,
those who've had a little seasoning,
invited to recall
how it was way back,

where everything had an intensity
you don't get so much anymore.

Like breaking up
with first loves
and how it felt
when your heart
gets ripped
from an open gaping
hole in the chest
Mayan style.

Or when you graduated
and left home,
to get the freedom
to do anything,

before
realizing
stuff ain't that simple.

It reminds me,
thinking back like this,
of a year old cat
trying to hunt.

About how
it sort of knows
what to do
but doesn't realize
the moves aren't all there, yet,

so that when the stalking starts
and just before the kill
the bird always flies away

because the cat's making
them excited chirping sounds
and flicking its tail like crazy.

Elders
usually know better,

the point being,
not about how
dumb them youngsters are

but about how
the feeling you had
when the first love
or the all grown up thing happened,
was probably a lot like
the cat on the bird.

The most sublime
Wonderful feeling
there ever was.

All There Ever Is

So many
still think
this now
ain't it

when
this now
is really

all
there ever is

sense

the thing about ego
is that while you've
probably struggled
to protect
and nurture
and grow it,
on the view
that through self
lies freedom,

the truth
likely
ain't so pretty,

as the oh so delicately
constructed
cage
its all become
comes into view.

For the lucky brave ones
who reach out
instead of shrinking away
to nothing,

there is the mere chance
to find truth
and finally know
what love
really is.

As always,
of course,
an asterisk appears
at the end of
the punch line,

to the effect
that these words
aren't it

and until
you really do
whatever it takes
to snuff out
the fetish
of self

no mere words
make the least
of sense,

and likewise
afterwards
are no longer
required.

Always Doing Being We Live Our Lives

Before I stopped drinking
I thought the world sucked
and the only thing that made sense
was rum.

When I stopped drinking
I thought the world was fine
but I sucked,
and the only thing that made sense
was sobriety.

Now that I am down that road a piece
I think the world is fine and so am I,

though its not that I'm all that
and a bag of chips,

because the truth is
that I ain't much different
than I was before.

And, while I once hated being a drunk
and was ambivalent at best
regarding this here recovery thingy,

it now seems more right
to be grateful for the booze
and its absence,

without which

I'd likely still be plodding along

with closed eyes

the same old way

I was before,

or worse.

I turned fifty this year. When I was a little kid, I wondered what that would be like. It was a foolish endeavor, chock full of dreamlike fantasies of rock stardom or being an important person. This was the early seventies. I lived on the trailing cusp of the baby boom where a pervasive sense of futility prevailed, as the childlike optimism of the former decade gave way to meaningless drug use and escape for its own sake.

In Buddhism there is talk of the Realm of Hungry Ghosts, a world populated by beings whose insatiable desires are thwarted by an inability to satisfy their cravings. It is not a happy place, as many in my generation can attest. No quantity of drugs, sex, stuff, therapy, career, or religious escape quenches our thirst.

I tried, though. I was a pot head, a social worker, an alcoholism counselor, a biker, a lawyer, a musician, an Episcopalian, a philosopher, a political candidate, a carny, a campaign staffer, an alcoholic, a pancake cook, and a husband (twice) and a father (once). I've lived in 14 towns in seven States, with five different women. Each chapter had its moments, but like any bad novel, the end never satisfies whatever hopes you held when the book was opened.

My teacher's teacher, Katagiri Roshi, used to talk about being in a corner where you can't move an inch. He spoke of how in that moment there arises – perhaps for the first time ever – a true opportunity to experience real silence. And, in that place, where its just you and your demons, there is a real chance for real change.

On the Fourth of July, 2004, I found myself in that corner. I had a moment of clarity, and the beginnings of a psychic change.

I started writing poetry in the Fall of 2005. The words have poured out in huge chunks, with no end in sight, leading to my first book, This Now, and these twin collections, Always Doing Being We Live Our Lives, and The Only Universe I Have Ever Known. Together they comprise a memoir of sorts, a running commentary on these last fifty years. I didn't get to be a rock star; I'm not an important person. I don't even remember all that much about what it was like being that kid way back when, wondering what the future held.

But I do know about the realm of Hungry Ghosts. I understand what it means to always need to change how I feel. I'm able to see the outlines of the corner where you can't move an inch. And for whatever reason, I find myself writing poems about it all.

Taiyu John Robertson
October, 2007

For David, Shoken, the Sangha, and everyone who has shared even a small piece of their recovery with me.

Impermanence is swift; practice with diligence.

www.ingramcontent.com/pod-product-compliance
Lightning Source LLC
Chambersburg PA
CBHW032103080426
42733CB00006B/403